CLARINET CONCERTOS
Nos. 1 and 2
in Full Score

CARL MARIA von WEBER

D1285871

DOVER PUBLICATIONS, INC.
Mineola, New York

Bibliographical Note

This Dover edition, first published in 2005, is a republication of Carl Maria von Weber's two clarinet concertos in one volume, originally published separately by Ernst Eulenburg, Ltd., Berlin (n.d.).

International Standard Book Number: 0-486-44628-X

Manufactured in the United States of America
Dover Publications, Inc., 31 East 2nd Street, Mineola, N.Y. 11501

Concerto No. 1 in F Minor
for Clarinet and Orchestra
Op. 73

Concerto No. 2 in Eb Major
for Clarinet and Orchestra
Op. 74

INTRODUCTION

Carl Maria von Weber's (1786–1826) two clarinet concertos appeared at a crossroads in the history of the instrument. Evolved from the single-reed *chalumeau*, the clarinet began to make an appearance in the orchestra in five of Haydn's twelve *London Symphonies* (1791–1795) and was sparingly used by Mozart in his later symphonies. Its timbres and orchestral possibilities made the clarinet a welcome addition; however, it wasn't until Mozart penned his final concerto for the instrument (K.622) a few months before his death in 1791 that the clarinet gained greater acceptance in musical and public circles.

Mozart and Weber both turned to the foremost clarinetists of their day for inspiration: Anton Stadler (1753–1812) and Heinrich Baermann (1784–1847), respectively. Weber met Baermann in 1810 while on a concert tour in Darmstadt and wrote his *Concertino* (Op. 26) for him. The two performed the work for King Maximillian of Bavaria, impressing him so much that he immediately commissioned the two concertos contained in this volume. The first concerto in F minor was composed in April and May of 1811 and premiered in Munich the following month on June 13. The second concerto in Eb major was written immediately after the first and premiered in Munich on November 25 of the same year. Weber wrote in his diary that the second concerto was met with "frantic applause, owing to Baermann's god-like playing."

While the crowd was won over, even the "frantic applause" was not enough to win over a publisher at the time, most of them still unconvinced of the instrument's potential and mass appeal. After Weber's opera *Der Freischütz* brought him widespread fame in 1821, publishers took a chance on his clarinet works. The two concertos were first published in 1822 by Schlesinger and designated as Op.73 and 74, although Weber listed them as Op.72 and 73 in his personal catalog. The risk was well worth it, as both works quickly joined the canon of clarinet repertoire.

Concerto No. 1 in F Minor

Instrumentation

2 Flutes—Flauti
2 Oboes—Oboi
2 Bassoons—Fagotti

2 Horns in F—Corni in F
2 Trumpets in F—Trombe in F

Timpani (tuned to F and C)—Timpani in F-C

Bb Clarinet Solo—Clarinetto solo in B

Violins (I and II)—Violini
Violas—Viola
Cello(s) and Bass(es)—Violoncello e Conntrabasso

Concerto No. 1 in F Minor
for Clarinet and Orchestra
Op. 73

Allegro   I   Carl Maria von Weber
(1786-1826)

1

3

5

6

7

*) So in der Solostimme der Original-Ausgabe! In der der Klavier-Ausgabe über gelegten Stimme dagegen:
Thus in the solo part of the original edition! However the following is superimposed on the piano score:

14

20

22

23

28

II

Adagio, ma non troppo

2 Flauti

2 Oboi

2 Fagotti

3 Corni in Es

Clarinetto solo in B

Violini

Viola

Violoncello

Contrabasso

Fg.

Cl.pr. (B)

Vl.

Vla.

Vc.

10.

Poco più animato

32

34

III

Rondo - Allegretto.

37

* Diese Taktzahl gilt für die Wiederholung.
This bar number applies for the repetition

38

41

48

49

55

64

350

71

Concerto No. 2 in Eb Major

Instrumentation

2 Flutes—Flauti
2 Oboes—Oboi
2 Bassoons—Fagotti

2 Horns in Eb—Corni in Es
2 Trumpets in Eb—Trombe in Es

Timpani (tuned to Eb and Bb)—Timpani in Es-B

Bb Clarinet Solo—Clarinetto solo in B

Violins (I and II) —Violini
Violas—Viola
Cello(s) and Bass(es)—Violoncello e Conntrabasso

Concerto No. 2 in Eb Major
for Clarinet and Orchestra
Op. 74

Carl Maria von Weber
(1786-1826)

I

81

84

150

100

103

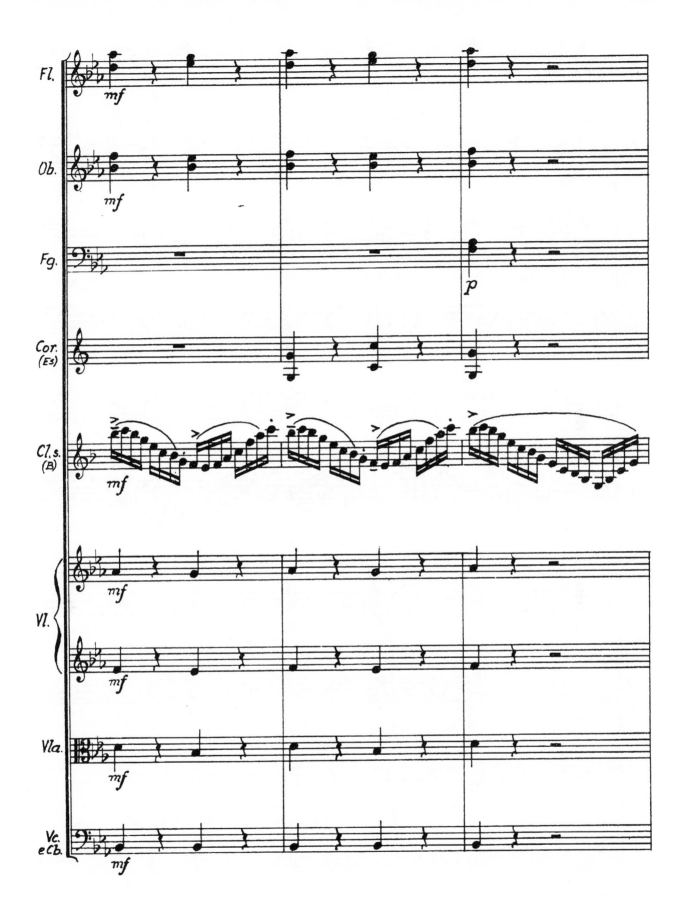

114

117

119

II

III

136

143

145

146

151

152.

159